WARWICK
THEN & NOW
IN COLOUR

LYNNE R. WILLIAMS

The
History
Press

In memory of my mother, Grace Thomas.

First published in 2012

The History Press
The Mill, Brimscombe Port
Stroud, Gloucestershire, GL5 2QG
www.thehistorypress.co.uk

ISBN 978 0 7524 6607 1

Typesetting and origination by The History Press
Printed in India

CONTENTS

ACKNOWLEDGEMENTS

My grateful thanks to the following for their valuable contributions: Paul (husband) for his enthusiasm and support, Grace Thomas (mother) for her memories, Vicki Riordan, Sheila Rouse (Mayor of Warwick 1980-1981), Stephen Wallsgrove, Les Kent (former councillor) the Warwickshire County Record Office and Warwick Library, *Leamington Spa Courier* Series (Warwick & Warwickshire Advertiser), Jo Cooper (technical advice) and David Oakley.

ABOUT THE AUTHOR

Lynne R. Williams has a a BA Hons in Social Studies from the University of Warwick. A keen traveller, she has visited Iceland, Norway, Finland and Switzerland where she has enjoyed snowmobiling, canoeing, white-water rafting and mountain walking. When she retired in 2007, she decided to research post-war Warwick as this particular time in the town's history had never been thoroughly recorded. She has enjoyed investigating local history for this new book comparing past and present Warwick.

INTRODUCTION

On the afternoon of 5 September 1694, the town of Warwick was ablaze. Rebuilding began soon afterwards in the style of William and Mary, in a manner that has commanded the admiration of many since. In 1716 Defoe said, 'It is now rebuilt in so noble and so beautiful a manner that few towns in England make so fine an appearance.' Now begin a journey through the years that shows how a small market and county town has arisen from the ashes and renewed itself post-war, whilst retaining its medieval central-street pattern.

Although the Great Fire destroyed about 460 dwellings, some of the older buildings, such as the Lord Leycester Hospital and the Beauchamp Chapel in St Mary's, survived. Warwick was fortunate not to experience the ravages of the Second World War which wrought much damage in nearby Coventry, however, it did not escape the wholesale demolition of many streets in the 1960s. Many of the buildings were seen as unfit for habitation and, driven by a need to improve public health, the Borough Council made rapid and radical changes that swept away austerity.

Inevitably there has been a loss of some listed buildings because of their poor condition, and town planning redevelopment in its earlier stages is typical of 1960s architecture, which is at odds with the essential character of Warwick. A notable example is the concrete-and-glass edifice housing the County Council offices, library and multi-storey car park, which sits astride the north-western approach to the town centre. This was hailed as brave new architecture but has been the subject of much criticism since.

The town walls have largely disappeared, however, Westgate and East Gate still survive as evidence of its defences, along with the impressive Norman castle to the south. Overlooking the river Avon, the magnificent castle is today a major tourist attraction which has put Warwick firmly on the map.

Major changes that have occurred over time have been the demise of manufacturing and family-owned businesses, and also family-owned individual shops. The small grocery shops, bakers, haberdasheries, fishmongers and furniture store have all disappeared, and in their wake came chain stores and supermarkets. The horse, sheep and cattle markets of yesteryear are but a memory. As a market town, Warwick still continues to hold a Saturday market in the Market Square, selling a variety of goods from foodstuffs to household articles.

Although the town has spread considerably from its compact and contained origins due to an expanding population, it still manages to retain a charm and timelessness in the streets that formed the cross: High Street, Jury Street, Castle Street, Church Street and Northgate Street.
We should not forget in our journey through time that a town is comprised not only of its buildings, but also its people. Warwick has been fortunate to have many benefactors, industrialists, entrepreneurs, architects, tradesmen and residents that have enabled the town to continue to successfully renew.

WARWICK CASTLE

GUARDING THE TOWN, the magnificent castle, built in the eleventh century, rises above the river Avon. Unfortunately, little of its medieval origins have survived and the castle we see today has had many alterations and additions. Most of these changes were carried out between 1743 and 1800.

The castle was the seat of the Earls of Warwick for many centuries, most notably Richard Neville, the King Maker. Described as the finest surviving medieval castle in the country, Warwick Castle was fortunate to be made the stronghold of the Parliamentarians during the Civil War and escaped the fate of other castles which saw them bombarded by canons and left in ruins. On display in the Great Hall is Oliver Cromwell's death mask, one of the fascinating relics from the 1600s.

It was first opened to the public on a regular basis in 1816 and is now one of the country's leading attractions. Madamme Tussauds acquired the castle in 1978, and has used its expertise to create waxworks displays, one of which depicts a royal house party in 1898, where the Earl and his wife, Daisy, entertain their distinguished guest, Edward VII.

The castle has been open to visitors since the end of the seventeenth century, and the initial trickle of visitors has grown to a flood. *(Photograph 1890)* *(PH47 3/26 Warwickshire County Record Office)*

THE CASTLE NOT only stands as a monument to Warwick's heritage, but also plays host to more modern events. Since the 1970s there have been Carols at the Castle. This event is held in the courtyard, and initially had glowing braziers relieving the darkness, which was wonderfully atmospheric. Sadly these had to be dispensed with as they created a safety hazard. A music festival is held in the grounds in the summer, culminating in a spectacular fireworks display. During the summer holidays other events include the firing of the giant trebuchet (a medieval catapult), knights jousting and falconry displays. It is interesting to note that in 1950, charges for entrance to the castle were 2s 6d, and 1s 6d for Warwick residents.

Warwick Castle provided the venue for a novel auction in 2009. The management auctioned the use of the castle and grounds for Christmas Day, beginning with a champagne breakfast, opening of presents under the Christmas tree in the Great Hall, Christmas dinner and a fireworks display. The winner paid in excess of £30,000. *(Photograph 2011 by L.R. Williams)*

MILL STREET

THIS CHARMING STREET with its Tudor buildings escaped the fire of
1694 and is a quiet and timeless backwater. When the old bridge that
used to connect Bridge End with Mill Street was destroyed and the new
bridge was built further upstream, Mill Street became redundant as a
main thoroughfare for traffic (horse-drawn wagons, tradesmen and
people entering the town) that once connected with Castle Street.

At the foot of the street is a superb view of the castle, dominated by
the magnificent Caesar's Tower. This was built between 1330 and 1360
with a unique double parapet. Rising 150ft, the tower had six storeys
which included three storeys constructed as family quarters, one storey
for ammunition and another as a guardroom. Beneath the tower is a
grim dungeon. Caesar's Tower was also known as Poitiers Tower because
of ransom money paid following the battle of Poitiers in 1356, which
probably partially paid for its construction. Prisoners taken were most
likely kept here. *(Photograph 1920s) (CR1125/94/10 images held at
Warwickshire County Record Office, photograph by A.H. Gardner)*

A MAGICAL GARDEN lies hidden behind the cottage to the right of the cottage in the foreground of this photograph, which has very fine views of the castle and Caesar's Tower, the old castle mill and the ruined bridge over the river Avon. The cottage garden, liberally planted with shrubs, plants and trees, occupies half an acre, and was created by Arthur Measures who acquired it in 1951. With winding paths, each turn reveals an awesome view. The beautifully tended garden appeals to all the senses: the rushing sounds of the mill race, birdsong, swans gracefully floating on the mill pond, lush greenery of trees, brilliant and subtle hues of flowers, scents and textures of plants. Arthur Measures so loved his garden that he wanted to share it, and through his benevolence it is open to the public for a small fee, the money collected being given to charity. A unique photograph opportunity is to be had by posing in the old stocks, however, throwing eggs and rotten tomatoes is strictly forbidden! In this tranquil setting it is easy to be lost in contemplation and gaze up at Caesar's Tower, wondering at the sights and sounds it has silently witnessed down the ages. *(Photograph 2011 by L.R. Williams)*

CASTLE HILL: THE BAPTIST CHURCH

THE FIRST AUTHENTIC record of the Baptist Church appears in the *History of the Midland Baptist Association* which was formed in Warwick in 1655, during the protectorate of Oliver Cromwell. The first Meeting House was built in the town around 1700, during the ministry of Benjamin Bowyer. This was later found to be too small and was demolished to make room for a larger chapel with a minister's house adjoining around the 1740s. The chapel was again rebuilt as shown in the photograph below, and opened in 1866.

To the right of the chapel, Oken's almshouses can just be seen. These were built in the sixteenth and seventeenth centuries by Nicholas Eyffler and Thomas Oken. The almshouses were modernised in 1958 at a cost of £6,700, and a bathroom and kitchen were added at the rear to preserve the picturesque frontages. Prior to this it was reported that six pensioners had to light a fire in the grate, with the wind whistling under an ill-fitting door, before they could get a cup of tea. During the winter months, in order to get the water for the tea, they were obliged to go outside and thaw the tap first. The pensioners were prepared to endure these hardships in order to maintain their independence in their declining years. *(Photograph reproduced by kind permission of Alan Skillicorn)*

THE MODERN BUILDING of the Baptist Church, with its architectural emphasis on clean lines and simplicity, is multi-functional. It illustrates the change in the church from a place solely for worship to a House Of God which is also used for community activities. The foundation stone of the new building was laid in 1998 with due pomp and ceremony by Mrs Sonia Hall, who had the distinction of being the longest-serving member. Next door, this enterprising church runs a cafe called the Gateway. Mainly staffed by volunteers, it serves delicious light homemade lunches, delectable cakes and a selection of popular coffees and other beverages. *(Photograph 2011 by L.R. Williams)*

CASTLE STREET – OKEN'S HOUSE

SITUATED ON WHAT formed the high cross of the street pattern in medieval Warwick, between Jury Street and High Street, lies Castle Street, home to the very quaint Oken's House. Thomas Oken, an Elizabethan benefactor, lived there until his death on 29 July 1573. In his will, he expressed a wish that the Trustees who administered his charitable bequests should hold a feast annually, and drink a toast 'to the pious memory of Thomas Oken and his wife, Joan,' and this is still carried out to this day.

Oken was believed to be the richest man in Warwick and made a fortune dealing in wool and woven fabrics. He was Master of the Guild in 1545, at the time Warwick was granted its town charter. When Henry VIII dissolved the guilds, Thomas Oken was one of the masterminds behind transferring the assets of the Guilds to the corporation and other charitable funds before they could be seized by the crown – a very wily and astute move. The charities he helped found are still active today. *(Photograph 1951) (PH210/182/6 images held at Warwickshire County Record Office, photograph by Philip Chatwin)*

SINCE 1955 OKEN'S House has served as a museum to what was claimed to be the finest collection of dolls in the country. The dolls were transferred to St John's museum in 2004 because the Council were of the opinion that the conditions in the Grade II listed building were a serious threat to their long-term conservation. Previously it had been a baker's shop, from around 1886 to 1909, and afterwards Grainger Brown's Antique Furniture business. The house has yet again been reinvented as a teashop, which is individually owned and serves a selection of teas and coffees in bone-china cups – a lovely nostalgic touch in this age of dishwasher-proof crockery.

Not too far away in the same street is the old dispensary. This was established in 1826 and was supported by voluntary contributions. It has functioned as a doctors' surgery and was used for the filming of the television series *Dangerfield* in the mid-1990s. Nigel Le Vaillant played the title role in 1995, followed by Nigel Havers in 1999. Next door is an eighteenth-century public house, Lanes, which had earlier been known as the Gold Cup, Richocchet and the Keep. (*Photograph 2011 by L.R. Williams*)

WESTGATE – LORD LEYCESTER HOSPITAL

THE WESTGATE AND Lord Leycester Hospital are a part of Warwick that has been held in a time warp, despite the passing surge of traffic that typifies modern-day Britain. Founded by Robert Dudley, favourite of Elizabeth I, for the charity of twelve poor brethren (old soldiers), it was licensed by an Act of Parliament in 1571. A far cry from its original use, this picturesque Tudor building has attracted the attention of many film makers and has been used for the making of television period dramas such as *Pride and Prejudice*, *Tom Jones* and *Moll Flanders*.

Westgate arch, constructed around the twelfth century, has a rather more ghoulish past. It was also known as a 'hanging' gate, and was a combination of church, toll-house and gibbet. The tunnel passing through was hewn partly out of the bare sandstone rock and was originally one of the only four entrances into the walled town. The passage is a substantial 84ft long and 13ft wide. The ceiling of this historic gateway is barrel-vaulted. A combination of the elements and passing traffic has resulted in erosion of the bare sandstone rock, and work has been carried out in the twenty-first century to buttress it. *(Photograph 1910s) (PH 352/187/246 images held at Warwickshire County Record Office, photograph by Henry Twigger)*

THE LORD LEYCESTER Hospital is still occupied by a master and eight brethren and their wives, although today their quarters have been modernised and are considerably more comfortable. Passing the Lord Leycester early in the morning, the brethren, clothed in their traditional 'blew' cloaks and hats, can sometimes be seen attending service at the St James Chapel surmounting Westgate. St James Chapel was built by Thomas Beauchamp, Earl of Warwick, and the tower was added in 1450. A little gem in this quaint Tudor building is the Brethren's Kitchen, which serves a tempting selection of cream teas, beverages and light lunches. A stroll around the pretty scented garden will bring the visitor to the remains of the old town wall. Peering over the wall to the left, nestling beneath the Leycester Hospital in Bowling Green Street, can be seen the four almshouses erected by the Misses Louisa and Julia Harris in 1889. The visitor might also find themselves accompanied by a startled chicken that has managed to fly over the garden wall from the adjacent garden. *(Photograph 2011 by L.R. Williams)*

THE HIGH STREET

THE GRADE II late eighteenth-century former Bear & Baculus Public House occupies the corner of High Street and Brook Street, adjacent to the Lord Leycester Hospital. The name was associated with the crest of the Earls of Warwick. This grand old building was saved from demolition by the vigorous protests of the Warwick Society, and is now a private house. The east wall of the building is timber-framed, now obscured by rendering. It contained a fifteenth-century ogee arched door or window head with chamfered jambs.

The old name for High Street is High Pavement, which comes from the areas in front of the houses which rise much higher than the road, where it was cut through the rock to bypass the West Gate. *(Photograph 1971) (CR2825 Warwickshire County Council: Department of Planning & Transportation, held at Warwickshire County Record Office)*

THE BEAR & BACULUS Public House finally closed for business in September 1970. It was fortunate to survive the demolition, which saw many of the old buildings in poor condition torn down before it was realised that they really should be preserved if possible. A report produced by Harold Mytum in 1975 pointed out that modern building techniques often destroy all archaeological deposits, and emphasised how standing buildings can add to our understanding of architecture and history. The Warwick Society was praised for its successful efforts to preserve buildings such as this. Now a private dwelling, it continues to enhance the High Street which has changed very little in appearance since it was rebuilt following the Great Fire of 1694, as shown in a drawing by W. Hollar around 1730.

The Great Fire started in the region of the Quaker Friends Meeting House on the opposite side of the street. It quickly tore through this central part of Warwick, destroying over 460 buildings, many of which were timber-built and thatched. It is easy to imagine the chaos and terror the fire created, however rebuilding quickly got underway and the stone-dressed buildings that emerged from the ashes are aesthetically very pleasing to the eye to this day. *(Photograph 2011 by L.R. Williams)*

THE HIGH STREET – THE WARWICK ARMS HOTEL

THE NOTABLE WARWICK Arms replaced a coaching inn burned down in the fire of 1694. In 1790 it was called the White Swan, and the street opposite, now called Swan Street, took its name from the inn. By 1834 the Warwick Arms was calling itself a hotel. It was once described as one of the principal inns, presenting a spacious front built of white stone in a simple, elegant style. It can also boast of accommodating Lord Nelson and Lady Hamilton in 1802. Bizarrely, the hotel was referred to as having Posting and Funeral departments in 1885. As can be seen from the photograph, parking in front of the hotel wasn't an issue in the 1920s when the volume of traffic was a mere trickle. (*Photograph 1921) PH143/575 images held at Warwickshire County Record Office, 'Copyright The Francis Frith Collection'*)

THE HOTEL IS well situated, occupying a prominent position on the High Street and being in close proximity to the castle. A fine portico adorning the front of the building was destroyed when a lorry reversed into it in 1939. As part of the war effort, the hotel was commandeered in 1941 and used as a Government Department until 1945.

The sign over the entrance is is reputed to be the oldest inn sign in the country, and shows a bunch of grapes.

Other businesses that were on the street for many decades included Lacy's, a stationers and printing firm established by Henry Lacy and later run by Mr Herbert. Henry Lacy's illustrated book, *Lacy's Threepenny Guide to Warwick and Neighbourhood*, published around 1923, can still be purchased. Also in the High Street was Gould's bookshop. Both of these businesses have long since disappeared. Moore & Tibbits, a firm of solicitors established in the 1800s, continue to ply their trade in the High Street, as does the firm of Godfrey Payton, Chartered Surveyors and Property Services Agents, established in 1806.

Another illustrious building occupying the High Street is Alderson House. This Grade II listed building's origins can be traced back to 1349/50, when the Earl of Warwick acquired the property from a John le Boteller. The building was purchased by Alderson House (Warwick) Ltd in 1961, on behalf of a number of Masonic Lodges based in Warwick. (*Photograph 2011 by L.R. Williams*)

JURY STREET

THIS IS A fine street between the West and East Gates, little changed since it was rebuilt following the Great Fire. These Edwardian ladies and gentleman on the flag-lined street could be anticipating the grand parade of the Warwick Pageant, held in July 1906 in the castle grounds and later described as 'the biggest thing which had ever happened to Warwick.' About halfway on the left, one of the most imposing buildings on this street was Jury Street House, which was built by Wagstaffe of Tachbrook, a wealthy landowner. This house is notable because the stone walls, half a metre thick, stopped the fire from continuing down the street and devouring the timber-built buildings beyond. It was owned by the Archer family until 1800, although by this time it had ceased to be used as a town house and was converted into the Three Tuns Inn. Part of the house is now incorporated in the Lord Leycester Hotel.

The Lord Leycester Hotel was the brainchild of the owner of The Warwick Arms, Arthur Henry Tyack, who bought 19 Jury Street in 1925 for £1,800, with the intention of converting it into a top-class hotel. It was opened in 1926. The motor magnate, Henry Ford, stayed here while visiting his factory in Leamington Spa. *(Photograph 1906) (PH672/33 images held at Warwickshire County Record Office)*

ALSO IN JURY Street, on the opposite side to the Lord Leycester Hotel, is the impressive building of the Court House in the right foreground. This was used as a court room from 1554, and also as a meeting place for the Corporation until 1590. The Mayor's Parlour was damaged in the fire of 1694, and, although the building was repaired, it was decided to rebuild it in its present opulent style in 1724. Francis Smith was the architect.

The Court House has continued to support social functions, and in 1951 provided the venue for Randolph Turpin to greet his fans from a top window when he won the world middleweight boxing championship. From the steps of the Court House, dignitaries have taken the salute from the Royal Warwickshire Regiment, and their colonel, Field Marshall Montgomery. The march past on Remembrance Sundays was usually led by the regiment's mascot, an antelope called Bobby, trotting out in front and being held firmly on a leash by his military escorts. No longer used as a court room, the Court House is now home to the Town Council, Tourist Information Centre and the Warwickshire Yeomanry Museum.

At the height of the 'mods and rockers' era in the 1960s, the popular El Ciento coffee bar on this street was greatly frequented by scooter riders and mods of the baby boomers generation, where, for the price of a coffee, they would 'hang out' listening to pop records on the jukebox for an entire evening. (No wonder the coffee bars declined!) The El Ciento was all the more attractive because it was regarded as a den of inequity by parents! From 1964-68 it became the Toreador and, afterwards, the Kingmaker, which lasted for about another twelve months. Today, the street scene, although often busy with traffic and pedestrians, is rather more sober. *(Photograph 2011 by L.R. Williams)*

JURY STREET – EAST GATE

STRADDLING JURY STREET and Smith Street, at the junction with the Butts and Castle Hill, is the East Gate to the town centre. This was one of the three gates which formed part of the defences of Warwick, and in medieval times was used for exhibiting severed heads on spikes. A far more grisly sight would have been the remains of the Catholic priest, John Sugar, who, after being confined for a year in Warwick gaol, was hung, drawn and quartered in 1604. Surmounting the archway is St Peter's Chapel which was built as a place of worship in the reign of Henry VI, and later converted to a charity school. The centre room was used for the education of boys, and a newly added wing built on the remains of the old town walls was for use by the girls. St Peter's was originally situated in the middle of the town but was demolished in the reign of Henry VI.

The building with a sign and black pot is the Porridge Pot Restaurant. This was formerly a medieval property which was refronted in around 1700 to match the style of other properties

built of brick and stone following the Great Fire. *(Photograph 1950) (PH352/187/184 images held at Warwickshire County Council)*

THE ADDITION TO St Peter's Chapel, built over the remains of the town walls, continued to be used by girls and became part of the King's High School. The Grade II scheduled Ancient Monument, built around 1420, was auctioned in 2010, and was purchased by an unknown buyer who has subsequently refurbished and converted it into exclusive rented holiday accommodation.

Beneath the chapel is the archway through which traffic used to pass until 1953. It was eventually closed because lorries would often get stuck when trying to pass through. A suggestion to put a portcullis at either end was summarily dismissed.

A tramline, running from High Street through Jury Street, passed around East Gate and continued down Smith Street towards Leamington Spa. In 1916, East Gate was the scene of a dramatic tram accident that occurred when a driverless tram left the rails and careered into the nearby Castle Arms. The driver had temporarily left the tram when a passenger alighted and trod on the floor-mounted bell push. Under the impression that the driver had rejoined the tram, the clippie released the rear handbrake, with catastrophic results. The three passengers were injured but, fortunately, not fatally.

The old Porridge Pot has been given a facelift and has been transformed into a Pizza Express. This was once a popular individually owned business. Alas, many of the individually and family-run businesses have disappeared, victims of high rentals for prime positions, having to compete with national chains and franchises. *(Photograph 2011 by L.R. Williams)*

23

SMITH STREET

THE CAVALIER PUBLIC House, formerly the Volunteer, was a fifteenth-century building with a modern facade in brick and fake timber framing. It was originally a three-bay house, with the central bay being an open hall which was later floored over. It probably served as a malting house during the sixteenth century. Malting houses in particular were mentioned by the justices, along with barns, stables and outhouses, as buildings that were consumed in the Great Fire of 1694. In order to prevent a repetition of the fire, the justices demanded that thatched roofs on some 200 barns, stables and

hovels be replaced with tiles. The total damage of the fire was estimated at about £120,000, which in today's figures would be over a staggering £180,000,000.

It is reputed that a tunnel ran from the Cavalier to the castle (an escape route from the castle perhaps?) To the rear were yards and a two-storey building with a cock-fighting pit upstairs and rows of terraced benches around it. A former landlord claimed that the pub was haunted, with the ghostly figure of a man in a wide-brimmed hat appearing at the window overlooking the rear. The pub was managed by John Francis and Sylvia Rose Plant from 1961, and Thornley Kelsey Breweries, who owned the property, sold the brewery and properties in 1968.

A once very popular watering hole in a street of thriving and diverse businesses, alas it is no more. (Photograph 1965) *(PH143/1195 reproduced courtesy of Warwickshire County Record Office)*

THIS IS SMITH Street following redevelopment of the former Cavalier Pub. Note that the Mock Tudor facade in the earlier photograph is missing. The street, which lies in close proximity to the castle, is still a hive of diverse small businesses. The street name was probably associated with the trades of goldsmith or gunsmith, which were typical of the smaller tradesmen and craftsmen found in any of the small market towns in bygone times.

The shops that thronged the street of yesteryear included Hardy's (furniture store), Peacock's (clothes store), the Co-Op (department store), Foster's (men's outfitters), Onion's (shoe shop), Boyce and Boy's (greengrocers), Carter's (gunsmiths), Davis (bakers), Bromwich (bakers), Hoffman (cobbler) and Tuckey (butcher). Although these shops have disappeared, the street continually reinvents itself with new businesses reflecting changing times and tastes. Today, these include different ethnic restaurants which are part of the diversity of the town. *(Photograph 2011 by L.R. Williams)*

ST JOHN'S

THE OLD COUNTY Cinema and former theatre was built about 1924, and closed in 1950. The proprietor in 1932 was C.O. Bretwell and the manager was W.E. Spriggs. It was succeeded by the Warwick New Cinema built further along the Emscote Road. Opening in 1940, it was said to be the most modern in Warwickshire. This, too, was closed around 1959 because it was losing money. It was usual in both cinemas for the screen projector to regularly break down, and this would be greeted with collective jeers and whistles from the audience. The hazy blue atmosphere of cigarette smoke would occasionally be penetrated by the beam of a torch flashed by the usherette as she guided customers to their seats.

The old County Cinema was subsequently taken over by Pickford's removal firm in 1960, and later sold in 1985. (Photograph 1980s) *(PH497/1 reproduced courtesy of Warwickshire County Record Office)*

RETIREMENT HOMES HAVE been built on the site of the former Pickford's removal firm, looking down St Nicholas Church Street towards the castle. This small, exclusive development of privately owned homes, known as

Castlegate Mews, occupies a prime position close to the castle, with shops in nearby Smith Street and St John's being easily accessible. At the far end on the right-hand side of the street is a select development of town houses built in the mid-1990s, which replaced the former Earls of Warwick Restaurant and Night Club. Out of shot on the left side of the street is St Nicholas Church, built in 1780. In 1800 there were a number of small, poor houses located opposite the church and near to the entrance of the castle. Rumour has it that when the King and royal family were coming to stay with the Earl of Warwick, these houses were purchased and demolished in a single day.

According to the historian William Field in 1815, a House of Templars was built between St Nicholas Church and St John's house by Roger de Beaumont, Earl of Warwick, during the reign of Henry I. The land belonging to the house included fields, meadows and pastures, as well as a water mill. *(Photograph 2011 by L.R. Williams)*

ST JOHN'S HOUSE

THE IMPOSING ST JOHN'S House was the Hospital of St John the Baptist, founded by William, Earl of Warwick, in Henry II's reign, for the entertainment and reception of strangers and travellers. The present mansion was built after the Reformation on the site of the old building. After the Dissolution of the monasteries in the reign of that larger than life monarch, Henry VIII, the land was passed to the Stoughton family. The house was rebuilt by Nathaniel Stoughton between 1666 and 1670, and looked very much as it does today. In its elegant lifetime it has served as a private school in 1791, and as a Record Office for the military during the twentieth century. From 1961 it has been used as a museum for the Warwickshire Regiment and, more recently, as a museum showing an authentic Victorian schoolroom, bringing to life the discipline and hardships endured

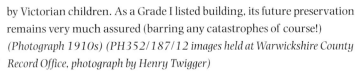

by Victorian children. As a Grade I listed building, its future preservation remains very much assured (barring any catastrophes of course!) *(Photograph 1910s) (PH352/187/12 images held at Warwickshire County Record Office, photograph by Henry Twigger)*

THE IVY CLADDING has been removed from the exterior, revealing St John's House in all its grandeur, complemented by sweeping green lawns on either side of the gravel drive. During the time it was being used as a Record Office for the military, a number of Nissen huts were erected at the rear and used by the staff. These were subsequently demolished in the 1950s and flats were built on the site overlooking St Nicholas Park. This small unimposing yet pleasant development is called St John's Court.

On the opposite side of the road to St John's House there once stood Brook House. This was occupied by Austin Edwards who ran a photographic film business in Coventry Road. Brook House was included in the schedule of buildings considered to be of historical and architectural importance. Sir Edward Ford, secretary of the Pilgrim Trust, had urged local authorities to take the long view and realise they were only temporary trustees of historic towns like Warwick. Proposals to demolish Brook House and build shops and flats on the site were carried out, despite objections from the Warwick Society. They had argued that the area incorporating the Crown Hotel, St John's House and the group of old houses leading into St Nicholas Church Street remained an impressive outpost of the historic centre of Warwick. *(Photograph 2011 by L.R. Williams)*

AVON STREET

THE WESLEYAN CHAPEL photographed in the process of demolition was first built in about 1849. It was rebuilt in 1863 and was still in use in 1965. The chapel was sold sometime between 1967 and 1969, and was subsequently demolished. The vacant plot was taken over by the nearby Industrial Mouldings Co. for their works. Further along the street, a row of charming bay-window-fronted terraced Victorian houses lend character and a quiet dignity to the area.

Avon Street takes its name from the lovely river Avon which flows close by and gently meanders through St Nicholas Park and beneath the castle walls. (*Photograph 1969*) (*CR1046/20 reproduced courtesy of Warwickshire County Record Office*)

IN THE 1970s and '80s a more affluent society saw an increase in consumerism and a rampant craze for do-it-yourself which took the place of the traditional Sunday worship for many. A Focus Do-It-All Super Store was built on the site of the chapel and former Industrial Mouldings in 1985. This building was the subject of much controversy as it was constructed two metres closer to the Emscote Road than allowed for by planning permission. Despite complaints, it was allowed to remain. This very unfortunate and crude corrugated-aluminium industrial construction mars the approach to the town centre on a road lined with some very fine examples of mid-Victorian houses. The building is now occupied by yet another national DIY store, Homebase, following the demise of the Focus-Do-It-All Stores in 2010. (*Photograph 2011 by L.R. Williams*)

THE BUTTS

IN TUDOR AND Elizabethan times it was customary for men to practise archery on Sundays so the name probably comes from the butts which were erected in this street for this purpose. It was known as Bachelors Butts until the mid-eighteenth century, and by 1837 was being used for the sheep fair. The College School, a large ancient building, was also located here. It has been described as a beautiful and interesting timbered house with a square courtyard in its centre, around which there were passages and rooms. When a new grammar school was built on the Myton Road in 1879, the old college was sold and subsequently demolished by the purchaser. This unfortunate act of what might be termed civic vandalism was greeted with general condemnation. St Mary's Vicarage is now what used to be the College School Deanery. The odd but interesting building shown in the photograph on the right, known as St Mary's Hall, also met the same fate in the twentieth century. It was previously known as the King's Middle School and also later served as a classroom for many years for the King's High School for Girls. *(Photograph 1960s) (PH143/119 images held at Warwickshire County Record Office)*

TODAY THE NEWER buildings belonging to the King's High School for Girls and adjacent flats are sandwiched between the fifteenth-century St Peter's Chapel at one end, and the grander Regency buildings at the other. The flats were built on the site previously occupied by St Mary's Hall, which was referred to by the Ancient Monuments Society as, 'eccentric but preferable to the proposed flats.' Mr John (Jack) Dean, a well-known proprietor of a painting and decorating business in Warwick, was educated here when it was the King's Middle School. Although childless, Mr Dean was fond of children, and on his eightieth birthday he threw a memorable party for a number of lucky youngsters at St Mary's Hall. This eccentric Victorian building, which lent character to the street scene, was nevertheless condemned and demolished in 1981.

Further along the street at the junction of the Butts with Priory Road is the Punch Bowl Hotel, a Grade II listed building that dates from around 1806. This pub also claims to have underground tunnels which probably connected with the castle. (*Photograph 2011 by L.R. Williams*)

CHURCH STREET:
ST MARY'S CHURCH

AT THE HEAD of Church Street, at its intersection with Northgate Street and Old Square, sits the reverential collegiate church of St Mary's, built at the end of the seventeenth century. It was established as a collegiate church by Roger Newburgh, Earl of Warwick, in 1123. The magnificent tower dominating the skyline rises 53m, and the breath-taking view from the summit is well worth the climb of 160 spiral stone steps. This illustrious Christian edifice is rated one of the best churches in the country and also boasts four choirs.

St Mary's also fell victim to the fire of 1694, after householders and tradesmen brought their smouldering goods to the church for safety, which subsequently set the church ablaze. The Beauchamp Chapel fortunately escaped the fire. It was built for Richard Beauchamp, Earl of

Warwick, who died at Rouen in 1439. The work was carried out to the highest standards by the best craftsmen obtainable, making it the finest chantry chapel in the country, surpassed only in size by the Henry VII chapel at Westminster.

Following the fire, the new church was built to the designs of Sir William Wilson of Sutton Coldfield, based on plans drawn up by Christopher Wren, although these were never fully implemented. Queen Anne contributed a munificent £1,000 towards it. *(Photograph 1920s) (PH143/428 images held at Warwickshire County Record Office, reproduced courtesy of 'Copyright Francis Frith Collection')*

CHARLES GUY FULKE Greville, Earl of Warwick, was laid to rest in the vaults of St Mary's, along with his ancestors, in March 1984. As a young man, the earl had tried to establish a Hollywood film career and adopted the stage name Michael Brooke. His career peaked with a supporting role in *The Dawn Patrol*, which starred Errol Flynn. Following his lavish funeral, the church was opened for the public to view the abundance of wreaths from his many famous Hollywood actor friends.

Church Street has changed little since it was rebuilt following the Great Fire, and the fine houses continue to grace the street almost exactly as they did in the eighteenth century. More recently there have been many occasions when enthusiastic crowds have lined the street to lend their support to processions, such as visits of Royalty, the annual parade of carnival floats, the march past of soldiers on Rembrance Sunday, the funeral of the Earl of Warwick, and the recent return of soldiers from Afghanistan. The deserted street scene of yesteryear has been transformed, and the recent photograph shows the street now lined with parked vehicles, another sign of the times. *(Photograph 2011 by L.R. Williams)*

NORTHGATE STREET

DESCRIBED BY ALEC Clifton-Taylor as 'the most handsome Georgian Street in the Midlands' in *Six More English Towns*, Northgate Street has always been what could be termed the better part of the town. The house nearest to St Mary's Church on the right hand side of this majestic street is the Judges lodgings, which was used as a residence for judges on circuit (judges who toured and heard cases in other towns), justices and the County Council. It was built in 1814-16 by Henry Hakewill at a cost of £8,000. Further along the row, the Shire Hall was built in 1753-58. This was completely refaced in 1948 with Hollington stone. The long, two-storied former gaol, designed by Thomas Johnson and built in 1779-83, completes the west side of the street. The cramped conditions in the gaol were far from humane and in 1860, on the advice of a more progressive

inspectorate, the gaol was rebuilt with better facilities on the Cape to the north of Warwick. The whole magnificent facade is completed with Greek Doric columns supporting an entablature with a triglyph frieze. *(Photograph 1920s) (CR1125/94/10 Warwickshire County Record Office, photograph by A.H. Gardner)*

ONE OF THE periodic events and a main attraction in Warwick was the pageantry of the grand procession of the High Court Judge, resplendent in wig and scarlet robes, followed by the judiciary and Warwick dignitaries as they left St Mary's and proceeded up Northgate Street to the Court. The traditional Assizes and Quarter Sessions were brought to an end in 1972 when they were replaced by the Crown Courts. After this point, it became unlikely that High Court judges would sit at the Court again, so this ceremony was discontinued, breaking the centuries-old custom which saw judges attending the preliminary service at St Mary's and being greeted by buglers. The Assizes and Quarter Sessions and presence of the county militia had previously brought great prestige to the town. In 2011 the court in the Shire Hall was closed entirely and transferred to a purpose-built judicial centre in Royal Leamington Spa.

The historic buildings on the left were once occupied by the County Education Department, and have remained empty and awaiting redevelopment since they were vacated by the department in 2007. The continuing deterioration of these grand aesthetic buildings has been the subject of much local concern. *(Photograph 2011 by L.R. Williams)*

MARKET PLACE

THIS VIEW WAS taken from Theatre Street, looking into the
Market Place after the demolition of the Rock Laundry. The
building immediately facing, with arches, is the Tilted Wig. This
popular hostelry was previously known as the Green Dragon,
Oken's Arms and the Kingmaker Public House. The arches were
once open for butchers' shops and in more recent times provided
welcome shelter for those waiting for buses. The pub now has a
continental ambience, with pavement tables, parasols and chairs
for customers to relax, eat, drink and watch the world go by.

The road featuring the car ran close to a small jitty where
small cottages once lined a cobbled street. Also in the jitty was
the Gospel Hall. These were demolished in the 1960s as part of
the slum clearance scheme. (*Photograph c1950*) (*PH143/732
reproduced courtesy of Warwick Record Office*)

IN THE FOREGROUND of the photograph is the statue to
one of Warwick's notable sons, Randolph Turpin. At the
age of twenty-three, Randolph won the prestigious title of

middleweight boxing champion of the world when he beat American Sugar Ray Robinson in 1951. Randolph trained at a local gym in the building of George Nelson Dale, under the direction of Arthur Batty, an employee of Nelson Dale and a well-known Warwick character.

Next to the Tilted Wig new businesses have sprung up in the wake of McBeaths the Chemist (later Mellor's) and Lloyd's Bank relocating to Swan Street. The national bookies, BetFred, now occupies the building once occupied by the Bradford & Bingley Building Society, next door is a cafe, and Lloyds' TSB has been replaced with Thomas Lloyd No.1, a fashionable bar. *(Photograph 2011 by L.R. Williams)*

MARKET PLACE

THE ABBOTSFORD WAS built in 1714 on the site of the Bull Inn and stands to the north corner
of the square. This prestigious building was designed by Francis Smith, son of a bricklayer from
Tettenhall, near Wolverhampton. Francis Smith was a surveyor at Warwick Castle in 1720-35, and
had earned a wide reputation for his buildings, which also included the Court House in Jury Street.
Immediately adjoining it is Walker Stores, one of the many shops that once surrounded the square,
including Johnson's on the corner with Old Square. Johnson's was particularly popular with the Mop
travellers, who bought bedding items there. The shop also displayed a wonderful model of the Mop in
the window. It later changed hands and became Owen's, a clothes shop, and today it is a newsagents
and wine shop. Also situated on the Square was the well-known family business Chris Jones,
fishmonger/fruiterer/greengrocers, but this too has long since gone.

Until the 1950s the square was virtually surrounded by two- and three-storey buildings, with
the Market House to the south being the only larger building. The buildings at the north end

were demolished at the end of the 1950s to make way for a large extension to the Shire Hall and a new access road by Abbotsford House, now called New Bridge, connecting with Barrack Street. Commenting on post-war changes in *The Buildings of Warwick*, Richard K. Morris said that some of these had been regrettable, mainly around the Market Square, which until the 1950s had been a proper country town square with a wide open space. *(Photograph 1938) (PH210/182/12 images held at Warwickshire County Record Office, photograph by Philip Chatwin)*

THIS GRACEFUL OLD building is now linked to the more modern Shire Hall via a glass bridge. It was refaced in 1985 and again in 2006, and later converted to stylish apartments.

The extension to the Shire Hall was built in the 1960s. Here, on the front above the entrance, is Warwick's famous emblem, the Bear and Ragged Staff. The Shire Hall was formally opened by the Queen Mother in 1966 amid much cheering and flag waving. The rather dull Market Place continued to be used as a bus and coach terminus and for car parking for many years. It was redeveloped in 1999, and further enhanced in 2003 at a massive cost of £1.3 million. The various aims of this costly project included making the square more attractive, encouraging more shops and entertainment venues to locate there. The bus and coach terminus was relocated at the foot of Market Street, and eventually a new terminus was constructed in Puckerings Lane. The free parking hitherto enjoyed by motorists was terminated as parking spaces were drastically cut and parking restrictions and charges implemented. York flagstones replaced the boring tarmac surface and huge flower planters were added, which has made the Market Place more cheerful and inviting. *(Photograph 2011 by L.R. Williams)*

MARKET PLACE

THE ANNUAL OCTOBER visit of the Mop Fair is an attraction that has always been the subject of much controversy. Originally a hiring fair for servants, the Mop is believed to have its origins in a Statute going back to the thirteenth century, when John de Plessitis, Earl of Warwick, was granted a fair for three days toll-free. The custom of people hiring themselves out as servants and labourers has long since disappeared, and these days it is operated as a Mop Fair with stalls and rides.

In 1901 the Court Leet recommended that the fair should be moved from the centre of town, or, failing this, that at least the livery vans should not be allowed and entertainment should cease by 11 p.m. In 1912 there was an attempt to confine it to Saturdays.

It was cancelled in October 1950 because the Showmen's Guild refused to agree to the increased Mop tolls of 4½d per square foot, introduced by Warwick Corporation. On receiving many letters of complaint from local people, the Borough Council resolved the matter and allowed the tradition to continue. Today, this time-honoured custom continues in its traditional place in the Market Square, despite efforts by the District Council to relocate it to the racecourse. *(Photograph 1928) (PH495/1 images held at Warwickshire County Record Office)*

IN THE PHOTOGRAPH above, the traditional Waltzers whirl around accompanied by ear-splitting music and screams of merrymakers. The helter-skelter towers in the background, while to the left are the blue poles of the new bungee jump. Traditionally, the Big Mop was followed by the Runaway Mop and was held on three consecutive Saturdays in October. The Runaway Mop was so called because if the servants who had been hired didn't like their new masters, and vice versa, they could return the following week and try their luck again. More recently this custom has changed and there is an additional Charity Mop. Originally, once it was erected the Mop was allowed to remain in the square and surrounding streets during its fortnight stay. This is no longer the case and it must now be dismantled and removed between the Mop 'going round.' *(Photograph 2011 by L.R. Williams)*

THE MARKET PLACE

LIVESTOCK MARKETS WERE held in various parts of the town, and as these gradually ceased to be held the Market Place became the venue for a weekly market in the twentieth century. No longer trading in livestock, the Saturday market is lively and bustling with a mixture of stalls selling anything from foodstuffs to household goods. The market has its origins in a Charter by Philip and Mary in 1554. Tuesday and Saturday were the appointed market days. The fountain featured in the photograph no longer graces the square. It was first erected to commemorate the visit of Queen Victoria in 1858, but by 1905 only the central plinth remained, the basin having been vandalised. The museum at the far end was originally a booth hall, built in 1670, with open arches for market stalls and meeting rooms above. In 1879 these were filled in as the museum expanded and was taken over by the Warwickshire Natural History and Archaeological Society.

Visitors to the museum today will be confronted on the first floor with the 9ft-high Russian bear, heraldic symbol of Warwick. The bear was shot in 1883 by a member of the Dugdale family from Wroxall, and was presented to the Warwick Natural History Society by Mr Frank Dugdale in 1912.

Also on the first floor is a fascinating model of Warwick as it was before the fire of 1694, together with an enthralling audio presentation of what happened when the fire broke out. *(Photograph 1951) (PH143/714 images held at Warwickshire County Record Office, photograph reproduced courtesy of Countrylife IPC Media)*

SHOPPERS LEISURELY PERUSE the wares on the market stalls on Saturday, while on other days the scene in the Market Place is one of relaxation as Warwick's cafe society spill out on to the pavement from the pubs and bistros. French, and farmer's, markets have become a popular feature in more recent years and are also held in the Market Square. A fairly recent custom that has been established for the past thirty-plus years is the popular Victorian Fair which takes place in the square and surrounding streets in November, attracting crowds eager to sample the delights of Victorian entertainments.

The museum was altered in 2010 to close the entrance, which was originally on the south side, and make a new one on the east. This was done to avoid the steps leading up to it and the obstruction caused by delivery vans. The easily accessible new entrance was created by painstakingly removing an arched window and replacing it at the site of the former entrance. The entrance now overlooks a paved area used by the nearby cafe, the Tuckery (previously Sensicles), and also market stalls on Saturdays. This area covers what was once the site of an underground public toilet. *(Photograph 2011 by L.R. Williams)*

MARKET STREET

A QUIRKY LITTLE street winding its way up to the Market Place, Market Street was once lined with a wide range of goods and produce shops, and was also the site of the Mulberry Tree Inn which closed in about 1907. A water tower was also located in this street. The most notable building was the Corn Exchange, a nineteenth-century edifice which was purchased in 1855 from the Castle Hotel and Excise Office which stood at the top of Market Street. It was subsequently demolished to make way for the Corn Exchange, designed by James Murray of Coventry. Plays were staged at the Exchange and in 1910 a license was granted to make use of it as a cinema. The Exchange Works was auctioned by Locke & England on 29 July 1952 at the Court House. The prominent clock on the Exchange Works was presented to shareholders of the Corn Exchange by Edward Greaves, MP in 1856.

Lower down the street, almost at its junction with Bowling Green Street, was Edward's Court, a small court of five houses. A little anecdote recalls that one of the tenants whose house fronted the street and had steps up to the front door was plagued with a nuisance being caused by local youths. It was the habit of the youths to sit on these steps to fraternise, and in order to discourage them the lady would pour a kettle of boiling water down the steps (history doesn't recall whether the lads were still sitting there at the time – this gives a whole new concept to being in hot water!). (*Photograph 1952*) (*EAC626 reproduced courtesy of Warwickshire County Record Office*)

IN THE 1950S/60s, businesses in Market Street included Miles (sweet shop), Jones (general grocers), Corbetts and Bartletts (bakers) Babettes (baby clothes), Wilkinson, and later Cartwrights (greengrocers), Ben Cowley (butcher), Megeney, later Franks (sweet shop) and Whittakers (fish and chip shop). These family-owned businesses were the hub of the community; the proprietors knew their customers well and gave personal service. In addition to purchases, a great deal of local gossip was exchanged in these shops.

The entire street was swept away by demolition, but the rebuilding of Market Street in the 1960s had its critics. Richard K. Morris in *The Buildings of Warwick* describes the wholesale redevelopment as, 'in a bland, untidy and confused late 1960s manner.'

Flats were built to accommodate an expanding population but the smaller businesses largely disappeared, being replaced by impersonal chains such as WHSmith and Woolworth's. Woolworth's was built on the site of the old Corn Exchange and closed in 2008. Its closure, caused by the collapse of the entire company, came as a complete surprise. Today, in its place, is a factory outlet and Costa Coffee Shop. (*Photograph 2011 by L.R. Williams*)

47

SWAN STREET –
THE WOOLPACK HOTEL

THE EIGHTEENTH CENTURY hotel was said 'to be well frequented by travellers and one of the principal inns at which the post office was established.' By 1850 it was running a Saturday carrier service to villages which included Long Itchington, Loxley, Snitterfield, Stretton-on-Dunsmore and Wellesbourne. From 1888 to 1892 the service had increased and, besides Saturday services, also ran on Tuesday.

Adjoining the Woolpack was the White Horse which stood on the corner with Market Street. This pub changed its name several times. In 1808 it became the Horse & Farrier, and in 1815 the

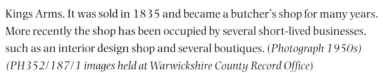

Kings Arms. It was sold in 1835 and became a butcher's shop for many years. More recently the shop has been occupied by several short-lived businesses, such as an interior design shop and several boutiques. (*Photograph 1950s*) (*PH352/187/1 images held at Warwickshire County Record Office*)

THE WOOLPACK HOTEL, along with other coaching inns, had lost its coach services by 1874. Horse-drawn omnibuses had become the popular form of transport that ran from the Woolpack and Warwick Arms, and these met all trains arriving at Warwick station. In 1881, nine omnibuses ran each day to Leamington, and the Leamington & Warwick tramway began to provide a service with horse-drawn trams running from High Street, through Smith Street and Coten End to Leamington. It was one of the smallest tramways in the country, running just over three miles. These were replaced by electric trams in 1905 and this service continued until 1930 when it was succeeded by the Midland Red Bus Co.

In 1957/58, £20,000 was spent on making the Woolpack Hotel one of the most attractive of its kind in the area. The historic eighteenth-century hotel finally closed in 1987. Grand plans to turn it into a shopping mall were eventually shelved in favour of a conversion to flats with one or two shops. The basis for this decision was in part to ensure the market wouldn't become a deserted area once the shops had closed. (*Photograph 2011 by L.R. Williams*)

SWAN STREET

ON THE CORNER of Swan Street abutting New Street is a fine timbered building dated 1634. This historic building was fortunate to escape the Great Fire and has since played host to a variety of businesses. In 1892 it was the Shakespeare Restaurant and for many years was the Beehive, a clothes shop and haberdashery. It was later occupied by Lunn Poly Travel Agents and today is Thornton's card and gift shop. A curiosity on the timber framing on the corner of this building above head height

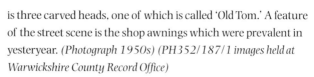

is three carved heads, one of which is called 'Old Tom.' A feature of the street scene is the shop awnings which were prevalent in yesteryear. *(Photograph 1950s) (PH352/187/1 images held at Warwickshire County Record Office)*

THE STREET SCENE has changed since the previous photograph. A building beyond the low three-gabled, timber-framed building of Mellor's the Chemist was demolished in 1951 and another erected. During demolition a fascinating discovery was made, yet another connection with Warwick's Parliamentarian past. This was a Civil War pass and letter dated 31 January 1644. At the far end of the street, on the left and out of shot, are buildings replacing the former Thacker & Christmas general grocer's corner shop. Thacker & Christmas was well known for its aromatic and heady smell of ground coffee beans being roasted, which wafted over the street. An antique centre now occupies the site, one of many antique shops for which Warwick has become well known. Today, the street scene is marred by the plethora of street furniture. *(Photograph 2011 by L.R. Williams)*

SWAN STREET

OCCUPYING AN IMPORTANT corner position between Swan Street and Brook Street, Mundy's was a family furniture and door shop that served Warwick for many decades during the twentieth century. In the post-war era it shared the street with a variety of shops that included Hanson's (records and later suede and leather goods), Ball's (chemist), Perk's (grocers), Chadburn's (butchers and delicatessen), Margaret Hall (cake shop), Bromwich (greengrocers), Sleath's (shoe shop), the Co-Op (grocers), the Red Lion (public house), Simm's (electrical goods), Vaughan's (toy and cycle shop), the Beehive (clothes shop/haberdashery), and last but not least, Thacker & Christmas (grocers). *(Photograph 1971) (CR2825/65 Warwickshire County Council: images held at Warwickshire County Record Office)*

A MORE AFFLUENT era has seen the demise of the small individual and family-owned businesses that thronged the street of yesteryear. The premises once occupied by Mundy's now houses Caffé Nero, a chain of coffee shops throughout the country and reminiscent of the old Lyon's corner

tea shops. A flourishing cafe society thrives in Warwick with its many coffee houses, pubs, gastro pubs, cafes, bistros and restaurants, and is a reflection of the changing times. Businesses now lining Swan Street include Mellor's (chemist), an established business that was originally located in the Market Square, Claridge's (stationery and cards), Warwick Sports Shop, Gregg's (savoury pastries, cakes and bread), Lloyds TSB, also originally in the Market Square and now occupying the building of the former Red Lion Public House, Present Days (gifts and clothes), the Cabin (newsagents) and Thornton's (card and gift shop). Also thronging the street is a variety of tempting eateries. *(Photograph 2011 by L.R. Williams)*

BOWLING GREEN STREET

THESE NINETEENTH-CENTURY terraced houses formed part of a street with other cottages that had a communal yard. Communal yards with outside lavatories and water taps were very common. This shared amenity often meant neighbours had very close relationships and there was a real sense of community. In this particular street, cottages were occupied by members of the Kent, Keen, Smith and Caulfield families. In pre- and post-war days it was usual for the extended family to live together, either in the family home or in very close proximity to it. This was a useful way of sharing the responsibility of looking after children and didn't entail the expense of placing small children in nurseries or child-sitting as it does today. The street was also much quieter in the 1950s/60s as car ownership was very limited. A favourite pastime was spotting car number plates and children would stand at the bottom of the street, at its junction with West Street, busily scribbling in notebooks. They played out in safety, either in the yard or the street and were imaginative in their games. No computers or Nintendos then! *(Photograph c. 1950) (PH202/1 reproduced courtesy of Warwickshire County Record Office and the Warwick Society)*

TODAY WE SEE a very different view. The old buildings were swept away in 1963 as part of a street-widening scheme. The white building beyond the new buildings was the only dwelling to survive demolition because of its Grade II listed status. This was the old forge which was once occupied by Frank Harrison, a whitesmith. Mr Harrison was responsible for repairing the clock on St James Tower, Westgate, and also made the weather vane surmounting the tower. To the rear of these buildings is part of the old town wall which bounded Warwick, and on the other side of the wall is the sixteenth-century Lord Leycester Hospital, founded by Robert Dudley, Earl of Leicester. Opposite these buildings is Westgate Primary School, built in 1884. Beyond the forge are the Guild Cottages almshouses, built in 1992 by the Charity of Thomas Oken and Nicholas Eyffler, founded in 1571. Missing from the street scene are the peacocks which were once regular visitors from the nearby castle. Sadly, the now constant deluge of traffic, a feature of modern-day Britain, has driven them from their usual haunts. (Photograph *2011 by L.R. Williams*)

BOWLING GREEN STREET

THE METHODIST CHAPEL and Sunday School was also used as a classroom and dining hall by Westgate Primary School. The house immediately next door was occupied by members of the Kent family. When members of the Methodist Church put on plays and concerts in the chapel, Mrs Ellen Kent supplied props (settee and chairs) from her front room. The chapel and terraced houses were demolished in 1963 as part of a street-widening scheme.

On the opposite side of the street to the chapel stood the old Bowling Green Inn which actually had a bowling green at the rear. The eighteenth-century Grade II listed building was transformed and reopened as the Westgate Arms Hotel in 1965, which closed for business in the late 1980s. The hotel was later converted into a development of thirty-eight luxury apartments and four townhouses. The development at the rear known as Martinique Square was built in the grounds of the hotel. This conversion attracted much controversy as it was feared traffic entering and

exiting the complex would prove a danger to children attending Westgate School next door. *(Photograph c. 1960) (CR1046/21 reproduced courtesy of Warwickshire County Record Office)*

THE DEMOLITION OF the Methodist Chapel, Puckerings Lane and Edwards Court in the 1960s cleared the way for a new road. This enabled traffic to pass directly from Bowling Green Street into Puckerings Lane and Brook Street. Previously, Puckerings Lane was a narrow jitty accessible only by foot. An archaeological dig was carried out on the site before building began and signs of Neolithic activity were discovered. Fragments of clay pipes were also found, originating from a nineteenth-century tobacco pipe factory which was located approximately under the walkway in front of the Saffron Restaurant. Shops and offices were built on the site of former Edwards Court and Puckerings Lane. Westgate House, housing the Health Authority, was built around 1972/73 and other businesses in this row now include Boots the Chemist, the Saffron Restaurant, M&S Simply Food and Heaphy's Gentleman's Outfitters. *(Photograph 2011 by L.R. Williams)*

WEST STREET

No. 16 WEST STREET was a seventeenth-century, or even earlier, building which had been drastically altered. It was once occupied by the Bell family and was also previously a grocery shop run by Mr Jelley. Mr Jelley also owned Jelley's Chapel which was formerly located in Leycester Place, close to the Lord Leycester Hospital. The graffiti on the hoardings is particularly interesting because it refers to a title track released in 1969 (Out Demons Out) by the Edgar Broughton Band, a local rock group formed by the Edgar brothers, also known as Rob and Steve Broughton. The torn flyer on the building advertises the James Brothers circus.

In 1830, West Street was described as 'wide and airy' and consisted of low houses inhabited by the working classes. The street retained its medieval proportions until the beginning of the

nineteenth century. Today, it still retains some of its old buildings and, now furnished with shops from takeaways to florists and ironmongers alongside the more recently built townhouses and flats, could still be described as 'wide and airy.' The new buildings interspersed with the old buildings lack individuality, being uniform in height and design, but nonetheless present a pleasing aspect. *(Photograph 1971) (CR2825/148 Warwickshire County Council: Department of Planning and Transportation. Held at Warwickshire County Record Office)*

THE POOR CONDITION of No. 16 saw it condemned as unfit for habitation despite its historic significance, and it was subsequently demolished. Three townhouses were built on the site and, although much smarter in appearance, they do not sit with the neighbouring building (previously a post office) quite as kindly as the former architectural eccentricity. Other businesses sharing the street that have long since departed were the Willow Cafe run by Mrs Guinness, and the hairdressing salon run by her daughter June, Vin Smith's general store, Talbot's fish and chip shop and Hope's newsagent. A memorable recollection of the 1950s was the ability to purchase a threepenny cone of chips. Fish and chips always came wrapped in newspaper – a thrifty bit of recycling. *(Photograph 2011 by L.R. Williams)*

WEST STREET

FURTHER ALONG THE street, the well-established businesses of Provitt's general grocery store and Elliot's the butchers have also been demolished and replaced with flats in the 1990s. Both of these businesses were typical of a small customer-friendly shop where the shopkeeper knew his clients well, nothing was too much trouble and shoppers were content to while away the time chatting. Tills that automatically added purchases and calculated change were not used here and the mental agility and deftness of the shopkeeper in calculating and wrapping purchases was quite a marvel to behold. Another feature of their heyday was the brown paper used for wrapping parcels and string. All wrapping materials in those days were recyclable as plastic bags were not available. *(Photograph 1973) (CR2825/66 Warwickshire County Council; images held at Warwickshire County Record Office)*

THESE SMART THREE-STORIED flats have been constructed to give a more
symmetrical appearance to the street scene. A few yards from Provitt's, another
very well-known general stores, Vin Smith's, flourished for many years. During the
1950s/60s coaches passing through Warwick would often stop outside the shop and
Mr Smith would hop on with a selection of ice creams which he sold to the captive
customers. On one particular Sunday the coach driver decided to play a little joke on
Mr Smith and closed the coach door to prevent him from disembarking. He carried
him all the way down Smith Street before releasing him!

Recalling a bygone era is the stalwart business of Torry's, now under new
management but retaining the name which had become famous for miles around.
This popular hardware and ironmongers shop next to the old passageway linking
West Street with Monks Way, has served the town for many decades. To dive into
its dark recesses was a nostalgic recollection of times past with its clutter of wares
displayed with utter abandonment. More recently the interior has been given a
thorough overhaul with a more thoughtful presentation of goods.

In this treasure trove it is still possible to buy single screws, nuts and bolts, and to
find necessary replacements for discontinued items elsewhere. (*Photograph 2011
by L.R. Williams*)

WEST STREET

THIS LATE EIGHTEENTH-CENTURY building was originally a barn with stables. It was later converted to a business establishment by Frederick Freer, seller of canvas goods and bunting. Notably, some of the windows used in this building came from the gaol, a massive Victorian edifice dominating the north of Warwick until 1934 when it was demolished. Originally located in Smith Street, the business moved to the West Street premises where it remained for sixty-eight years. Founded in 1835, it had the distinguished record of being one of the few surviving family businesses in Warwick run by grandsons Kenneth and Stuart Badger. The firm relocated to Emscote Mills, Wharf Street in 1999. High points in their trading career included supplying marquees for the sumptuous wedding celebrations of Lady Diana Spencer and Prince Charles at Althorpe House in 1981, and also items for the television drama series *Dangerfield* which was filmed in Warwick. *(Photograph 1973) (CR2825/66 Warwickshire County Council: images held at Warwickshire Record Office)*

WITH THE DEPARTURE of Frederick Freer from these premises, the building was converted into a small housing development and is now called Tanners Courtyard. The facade has been preserved, as can be seen from the earlier photograph.

To the right of this building, a little further along the street, was Jack Taylor's, a popular transport cafe noted for its colourful exterior which, alas, has been painted over. It is now the Antiques and Work of Arts emporium. Also to the right is a new housing complex, Charter Approach, which was built on the site of the former engineering works, the Improved Hinges. In 1958, the Improved Hinges was sole supplier to British Rail for carriage doors and hinges. Founded in 1936 with twelve employees, by 1958 the workforce had increased to 300 and the floor space was doubled. Improved Hinges was based in Warwick for about seventy-five years and relocated to Broxell Close in the mid-1990s. It was then producing interior hinges for cars. The factory closed around 2001. *(Photograph 2011 by L.R. Williams)*

CROMPTON STREET

THIS STREET WAS first rated in 1825 and formed the western suburb of Warwick along with Woodhouse Street, Stand Street, Hampton Street, Queens Square, Monks Street and part of lower Friar Street. An expanding workforce needed to be accommodated, and by 1851 these streets were closely packed with back-to-back houses and interspersed with inns and skittle alleys, the only industry being the foul-smelling tannery of Samuel Burbury. Although, by this time the major manufacturing industries such as the woollen, cotton and lace industries had declined, the building of the canal had brought new industries to the town and the population was expanding.

About halfway along on the south-west side is the quaint Old Fourpenny Shop. The origin of this pub was first mentioned by Thomas Kemp in *A History of Warwick* as the Paul Pry built in the 1790s. Apparently the pub took its name from a horse called Paul Pry. Crompton Street did not exist when the original inn was built with stables for the purpose of serving the racecourse. The pub later became the Warwick Tavern when the street was built, then changed to the Old Fourpenny Shop, and it is now called the Old Fourpenny Shop Hotel. (*Photograph 1949*) (*PH143/497 reproduced courtesy of Warwickshire County Record Office*)

CROMPTON STREET HAS the distinction of supporting three public houses: the Foresters Arms at one end and the Wheatsheaf Hotel (also now called Mr India) at the other, with the Old Fourpenny Shop Hotel in the middle. The Old Fourpenny Shop, along with its sign, is visible on the left. It was so called because during the building of the Warwick section of the Grand Union Canal in the early 1800s, the charge for a cup of coffee and tot of rum was four pennies. At the far end of the street is the open aspect of Warwick Racecourse. The herdsman's cottage at the entrance shown in the old photograph has been demolished. A planning application was put forward by the Jockey Club in 2010 to build a 100-bedroomed hotel at the racecourse entrance, which would obscure this lovely open view and, needless to say, attracted a great deal of vociferous local opposition. (*Photograph 2011 by L.R. Williams*)

WOODHOUSE STREET

WOODHOUSE STREET WAS first rated in 1827. The small terraced houses were built
back-to-back and little heed was paid to the need for individual space. Large extended families
would often be huddled together in one or two tiny rooms. The Parker-Morris Standards, which
identified the need to design housing providing sufficient space to swing a cat in, was to come
much later after the Second World War. They were introduced in the late 1960s and became
mandatory for all council-housing building. The Victorian and Edwardian populations would
have been surrounded by plenty of green open spaces, with the Common and Lammas Fields,
and pastureland between the Hampton Road and Stratford Road. This became urbanised in the

1950s with the building of the Forbes Estate between Hampton Road and Stratford Road, and later the Chase Meadow estate built on a green-field site beyond Gog Brook in the 1990s.

These older terraced houses looking towards Stand Street were demolished in the 1960s. (Photograph 1963) *(PH143/1332 reproduced courtesy of Warwickshire Record Office through W.T. Rhys)*

WHEN THE VICTORIAN terraced houses were demolished, the rows of neat modern terraced houses replacing them were built on the same footprint. The frontages are each complemented by a small, low-walled garden which enhances the street, providing a cheerful exterior to the properties. A corner shop at the top of Woodhouse Street and Crompton Street was run by Wallington's. This was demolished somewhat later than the rest of the street and was replaced with flats.

Woodhouse Street nearly became part of the route of a proposed inner relief road in the 1970s. The scheme to help solve traffic congestion in Warwick was abandoned by members of Warwick Town Council in 1970 because of new plans to build a western bypass. The route considered would have been via a roundabout at the junction of Stratford Road with St Laurence Avenue, cutting through Queen's Square and Woodhouse Street, across St Mary's lands to the Saltisford and swinging eastward across the Priory Park to a roundabout at the junction of Coventry Road with St John's. *(Photograph 2011 by L.R. Williams)*

FRIARS STREET

FRIARS STREET DERIVED its name from the Black Friars House which stood outside the town walls to the south-west. The Black Friars had settled in Warwick during the reign of Henry III, and the house stood somewhere opposite the spot now occupied by St Paul's Church. The Severn Stars was formerly the Cross Keys. Built in 1844, St Paul's was formed out of the western part of St Mary's parish and encompassed the original cemetery chapel built in 1824, known as St Mary's Episcopal Chapel. In 1855, burials in the church and churchyard were ordered to cease, except in the existing vaults and graves. An enclosed space near to the Common entrance in Friars Street also had historic connections. Bread and Meat Close originally derived its name from charitable works. In 1729, Nicholas Rothwell gave some land in Friar Meadow for the purpose of providing

bread and meat annually for the poor. This was to be distributed at the discretion of the Trustees. The charity was regulated in 1908 when it was administered by the Trustees of the United Charities and in 1956 it became part of the United Charities, of Richard Griffin and others. The annual income from the property, then used as gardens, was £28. *(Photo 1970) (PH143/526 images held at Warwickshire County Record Office)*

FLATS WERE BUILT on the site of Bread and Meat Close in 2006/07. This was previously the site of Merrall's Smithy and was also used as a car park and lorry park for the Mop on its annual visit to Warwick in October.

Former tenants in Friars Street included the Bartletts who were notable for producing two mayors of the town, Alderman 'Ted' and daughter Sheila. Next door lived the Haines family. Towards the top of the street on the right, Barbara Morris ran a second-hand clothes shop and the Cookes had a cycle-repair shop. Miss Cooke also ran a cycling club. Bill Kent, from Bowling Green Street, was a prominent member of the club in the 1950s, and organised many cycle races. As with other older terraced houses in Warwick, those in Friars Street were also swept away in the 1950/60s and were replaced with terraced housing, which this time included inside toilets and bathrooms. Older people's bungalows now occupy the site to the right of the Severn Stars, and to the left is St Paul's Church. This underwent a drastic alteration in 1978 when the interior was converted from an east/west to a north/south orientation. The east/west orientation was reinstated in 2001. *(Photograph 2011 by L.R. Williams)*

ST MARY'S LANDS

ARE THESE ELEGANT ladies and gentleman gathered around the grandstand anticipating a race or have they perhaps just witnessed one? The popular sport of horse racing at Warwick has its origins in 1707 when Lord Brooke gave £15 to the Chamberlains 'towards making a horse race.' Racing grew in popularity and a race stand was erected in 1809 and enlarged in 1852. Regular races are now held and continue to attract a substantial crowd. Far beyond the grandstand is Lammas Fields where the Victorian Gardens were located.

The Common and Racecourse are the more familiar names for St. Mary's Lands. The Commonable lands were originally gifted to the poor of Warwick in the latter half of the thirteenth century by Margery, widow of John de Plessitis, Earl of Warwick. The Common ground was called cleyputtis (clay pits) and the inhabitants of Warwick were once allowed to graze their animals on the Common. The Common is now in the ownership of Warwick District Council who bought the Common rights from the remaining Common holders in 1949. Very unusually an Act of Parliament does allow the many public footpaths across the racecourse to be closed on race days.

During an air raid in the Second World War, a German plane dropped a bomb on the Common, tragically killing two men who had left their works and were hurrying home to see if their wives were safe. *(Photograph 1914)* *(CR1618/WA16 images held at Warwickshire County Record Office)*

A NEW GRANDSTAND was built in the 1990s which incorporated what was the oldest grandstand in the country. The Common is now used for a variety of pursuits, which include horse racing, a golf course, model aeroplane flying, caravanning and walking.

Post-war proposals to build houses on the Lammas fields met with strong opposition. An old Warwickian, Captain E.G. Tibbits wrote, 'The Common is and has been a source of pleasure and health to hundreds of Warwick children and their parents and I fear once the process of whittling away parts of the common commences it will be continued.'

Hill Close Gardens, on the Lammas fields, were preserved as an important part of Warwick's history when a suggested development for up to fifty houses was opposed by the Lammas and District Resident's Association and English Heritage. The gardens were created as an enclosed area in 1845 to provide a place of relaxation for shopkeepers and others living over town-centre premises. Owners and tenants would visit the gardens on Sundays to tend their fruit and vegetables. A programme to restore the unique Victorian gardens and summerhouses has been completed and these are now open to the public. *(Photograph 2011 by L.R. Williams)*

THE HOLLOWAY

THE HOLLOWAY WAS part of the old salt way into Warwick from Droitwich, and traffic passed through it into the town centre from the Saltisford. John Rous, a fifteenth-century historian, records that there were some salt wells within a mile of the town. The Holloway was cut through solid rock and used as a major thoroughfare until it started to collapse, which led to it being filled in. The traffic was re-routed through Theatre Street. One of the more unusual forms of traffic on one occasion was a troupe of circus elephants and camels. The order to close the Holloway was made in 1975. *(Photograph 1971) (CR2825 Warwickshire County Council: images held at Warwickshire County Record Office)*

THE REMAINING PART of the Holloway is no longer a thoroughfare for traffic or elephants and is now lined with a diversity of businesses including Flo's, a sandwich shop which is very popular with local employees and businesses.

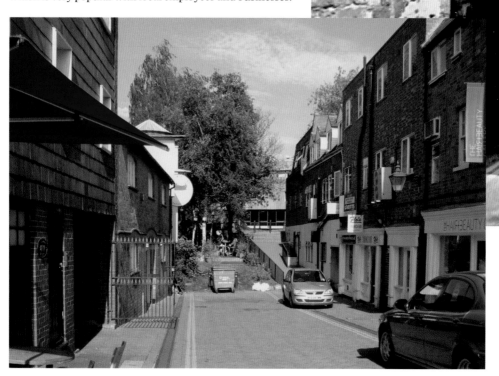

The litter bin pictured at the far end is unfortunately a permanent feature, but marks the point where the Holloway was filled in.

At the Market Place end of the Holloway stands the Rose & Crown Public House. This was first recorded in 1788. In common with the Cavalier Pub that was situated in Smith Street, the Rose & Crown is reputed to have underground passages that linked up with the castle. This lively little pub is part of a very cosmopolitan scene in the square today with its tables, chairs and umbrellas on the pavement during the summer season. *(Photograph 2011 by L.R. Williams)*

THEATRE STREET

THE GLOBE HOTEL is an eighteenth-century Grade II listed building, established as a public house in 1788 run by Tobias Edwards. It first acquired its name in 1888 and was converted to a hotel around 1908. The Globe had shared the street with the theatre which was demolished in the mid-nineteenth century and replaced with a slaughterhouse. The changing face of Warwick as a town with a historic heritage and yet coming into its own as a modern, diverse and vibrant place was seen with the transformation of this building into the country's first Thai-style hotel in 2002. *(Photograph 1973) (CR2825/148 Warwickshire County Council Department of Planning and Transportation. Held at Warwickshire County Record Office)*

SITUATED AT THE top of Theatre Street and New Bridge (previously Ironbridge), the Globe has undergone another transformation. Taken over by a chain in 2010, it has been renamed the Lazy Cow. In addition to the normal restaurant meals, they also serve breakfasts and a special weekend brunch between 7 a.m. and 12 noon. It must be said however, that the fibreglass cow standing in the forecourt of this grand old listed building does little to enhance it. An amusing and innovative signboard featured close to the cow invites ladies to park their men-folk in a husband's crèche where they will be well looked after for free until they are collected and their drinks bill paid for by their women! (A nice piece of harmless humour which thumbs its nose at political correctness.)

The customary hog roast on the Saturday morning of the Big Mop in October was usually held outside what used to be the Globe Hotel. Spectators gather round the glowing coals while the pig is turned on the spit, savouring the mouth-watering rich aroma. The Lazy Cow kindly donated the 'hog' in 2011. When cooked, the first slice is auctioned for the Mayor's charity, and the pig is then carved and presented in batches with stuffing and apple sauce and sold to salivating customers. *(Photograph 2011 by L.R. Williams)*

THEATRE STREET

HERE IS A rare glimpse from Theatre Street to the rear of the Market Square with the spires of St Mary's Church jutting above the roofline. As its name would suggest, Theatre Street was the site of a theatre and street entertainments. The theatre was demolished in the mid-nineteenth century and a slaughterhouse was built on the site. *The History of Warwickshire* records that a theatre to be put in the Market Place was planned by John Boles Watson, which he proposed to open for 'dramas' on race days and other public days. Unfortunately for Mr Watson it appears that his plans were met with considerable objections by the inhabitants of the Market Place, and Watson was forced

to return to his old shop, the theatre in Cocksparrow Hall. Cocksparrow Hall was located in the area between Linen Street (off Theatre Street) and lower Friar Street. *(Photograph 1971) (CR2825/146 Warwickshire County Council. Images held at Warwickshire County Record Office)*

FLATS NOW OBSCURE the brief view in the older photograph. Although the new building has been built to emulate the building on its right, it is a pity that details such as the lintels over the windows were not added and the proportions of the windows not copied.

A stroll along this side of the street brings the pedestrian to an archway and a flight of steps into the Market Place. The flight of steps is on the line of a mediaeval alley that led to a postern gate through the defences and out on to the Common. This cut-through to the market was previously a jitty, a cobbled street lined with humble little cottages and the Gospel Hall, and these, too, perished in the wholesale slum clearance scheme in the 1960s. A multi-storey car park erected at the junction with Linen Street in the early 1970s was referred to by the press as a 'white elephant.' This was because it was mostly empty at that time and therefore considered unnecessary, but it now provides much needed parking spaces for the town. *(Photograph 2011 by L.R. Williams)*

COCKSPARROW STREET – MARBLE HOUSE

SITUATED JUST OFF Theatre Street, a short walk down Cocksparrow Street reveals one of the most impressive houses in Warwick overlooking the racecourse. Marble House was built in 1650 and belonged to Humphrey Yardley, who sold the house and adjoining land, stretching from Linen Street to Parkes Street, to Francis Smith in 1724. The name is derived from Smith's marble mason's yard which occupied the site.

Marble House was subsequently acquired by William Parkes, a worsted cloth manufacturer, who increased the estate by acquiring the adjoining property to the north and built his woollen mill just off the Saltisford in 1776. Further notable occupants included the Molladys in 1850, who owned a hat factory in the town.

In one of the rooms a carving in the panelling shows a shield with the coat of arms of the Grants of Norbrook. This family was deeply implicated in the Gunpowder Plot in 1605. The panelling probably came from Norbrook, which was demolished about the time Marble House was built. (*Photograph 1903*) (*PH143/705 images held at Warwickshire County Record Office, reproduced courtesy of Countrylife IPC Media Ltd.*)

THIS GRAND, FOUR-STORIED Jacobean house was also home to Mr J. Tibbits and family. Mr Tibbits was a well-known Warwick solicitor whose practice Moore & Tibbits still has its premises in the High Street. The property was later converted into offices and, after falling into disuse, was acquired by the present owners in 2011, who have undertaken to restore it to its former glory. Building works have begun and a new porch has been added. (*Photograph 2011 by L.R. Williams*)

BARRACK STREET

THESE TWO LADIES are deep in conversation in front of the rather drab and depressing buildings that constituted the street scene of yesteryear. On the opposite side of the road the police station that once stood on the north side of Barrack Street, built on the site of the Bridewell, was demolished in 1972. The constabulary relocated to a new purpose-built police station at the top of Priory Road. This was built on the site once occupied by the gates of the Priory Lodge. A little road winding off to the north of this street was called Joyce Pool, where there stood a collection of humble cottages. These stood on the site once occupied by a very grand Jacobean house in 1663. Joyce Pool was demolished in the 1960s.

At the far end is Northgate Methodist Church. The 100-year-old building was demolished in June/July 1992 and rebuilt. The new facelift cost in excess of £300,000 and was designed to create as much multi-purpose space as possible. The orientation of the church was also changed from east/west (the usual orientation of churches) to north/south, and a new stained-glass window with a cross radiating shards of light overlooks the rear on the north Rock. The author's mother, Grace Thomas, was a long-serving member of the church, attending from early childhood into her eighties. *(Photograph 1930s) (PH210/182/2 images held at Warwickshire County Record Office, photograph by Philip Chatwin)*

BUILT ON THE site of the former police station and Joyce Pool is the Warwickshire County Council offices, library and multi-storey car park. This glass and concrete edifice looms large, and is a classic example of the 1960s brave new architecture. It has attracted severe criticism and was voted the third

ugliest building in the United Kingdom in a television poll in 2006. Sitting astride the north-west approach to the town centre, it obscures the view of the magnificent St Mary's Church with its soaring tower, which otherwise dominates the skyline. The library was previously housed in the building adjacent the War Memorial in Church Street, alongside the medieval footpath called the Tinker Tank, which connects with the Butts. The Abercrombie Plan for Warwick, adopted in 1950, intended that the redevelopment of Warwick would also ensure the preservation of many buildings and the sympathetic design of new ones. The erection of such an unsympathetic building has attracted much controversy, not least because of its close proximity to the regal beauty of Northgate Street and St Mary's Church. (*Photograph 2011 by L.R. Williams*)

WEST ROCK

THIS ROW OF houses sandwiched between
Theatre Street and the Saltisford was previously
called Alton Terrace. In the foreground, a gas
lamp is a stark reminder of the dimly illuminated
streets of yesteryear where the ghostly light barely
penetrated the gloom. Opposite is Ironbridge over
the Holloway. Ironbridge was erected in 1804
and consisted of one arch measuring 24ft and
was given to the town by Charles Mills, MP for
Warwick. It was demolished in 1975. *(Photograph
1950) (PH1035/B3089 reproduced courtesy of
Warwickshire County Council Museum Services. Held
at Warwickshire County Record Office)*

ALTON TERRACE, ALONG with Parkes Street
and Wallace Street, did not escape wholesale
destruction. Like other towns in Britain, the
post-war situation presented the Borough Council
with a challenge and an opportunity to make

radical changes which would sweep away post-war austerity and revolutionise people's living conditions and lifestyles. New homes were built to accommodate an expanding population in the 1950s, '60s and '70s. The Abercrombie Plan for Warwick, adopted in 1950, proposed that the long-term aim of piecemeal construction should be to preserve as far as possible the historical character of the area. Alton Terrace was renamed Oken Court after the town's famous benefactor. Today, this row of terraced houses and flats step smartly down the Rock, complemented by lush greenery. (*Photograph 2011 by L.R. Williams*)

THE ROCK

HERE IS THE Rock, following demolition of Alton Terrace. The County Offices, library and multi-storey car park dominate the scene and are in stark contrast to their surroundings. The junction between the Birmingham Road and the Saltisford to the left of the small island was the scene of many traffic accidents, despite a clear view. The island was later replaced with a roundabout. Beyond the island, on the Saltisford, is the Kings Head Inn a 400-year-old public house. A huge leap in time from its medieval origins, the twenty-first-century inn now offers free Wifi in addition to accommodation. At the top of the road is the Globe Hotel, now called the Lazy Cow. *(Photograph 1971) (CR2825/146 Warwickshire County Council. Images held at Warwickshire County Record Office)*

ALTHOUGH POST-WAR town planning was widely criticised and the wholesale demolition of historic properties condemned, this row of flats and townhouses built in the latter half of the 1970s is a splendid example of what can be achieved with good design. The County Council building and multi-storey car park has also been

improved in recent years with a screen of trees which hides the stark ugliness, although only from spring to autumn as the trees are deciduous!

A new road called Commaigne Close leads off Oken Court down a slope to a public car park, and Sainsbury's, which was built in 1985. This new road, lined with a mixture of flats and townhouses with a view over the racecourse, is on the site that was once occupied by Parkes Street and Wallace Street.

History records that a scaffold once stood on a site near to Wallace Street. Here on 2 April 1781 at 7 a.m. Captain John Donellan was executed for the murder of Sir Theodosius Boughton of Lawford Hall. (*Photograph 2011 by L.R. Williams*)

PARKES STREET

THE SCHOOLBOY HURRYING along the street sports a now unfamiliar school cap. The name of the street came from the brothers William and Joseph Parkes, who established a wool and cotton mill in the Saltisford in 1776, in partnership with Joseph Brookhouse and Samuel Crompton. Woollen and cotton manufacturing were staple industries in Britain during the late eighteenth and nineteenth centuries, and Warwick was no stranger to these. By 1815 the mill employed about 500 people. The chief markets for worsted were Leicester, Hinckley and Nottingham, and Kidderminster for yarn. By the mid-nineteenth century the woollen mill had declined and been replaced with other trades, such as Mollady's hat factory in the Saltisford, Robert's Iron Foundry in Coventry Road and William Holland's stained-glass and decorative painting establishment at St John's.

Adjoining Parkes Street was Wallace Street, the name of which had a very unusual origin. In 1825 a lion called Wallace was procured by William Wombell to fight bulldogs two at a time for the entertainment of onlookers. The fight was staged in a cage in an enclosed arena called Factory Yard, near to the Saltisford. Wallace excelled himself by killing two of the dogs, much to the satisfaction of the crowd. Unlike Parkes Street, however, the name of this

street wasn't kept, and slipped into oblivion when it was demolished. *(Photograph 1963) (PH143/917 reproduced courtesy of Warwickshire County Record Office)*

DRIVEN BY A need to improve public health, a post-war programme of slum clearance was embarked upon by the then Borough Council, which swept away the terraced houses. These would have had neither bathroom with running water nor inside toilets. The 1951 census records that less than half of the population had a fixed bath (48 per cent) while only 19 per cent had piped water to the building. Baths were taken in tin tubs, usually weekly in front of a coal/coke fire in the living room, or in the scullery under the dim light of the gas mantle. Coming forward in time, the cotton and woollen mills have long since disappeared, and the street rechristened Commaigne Close is now furnished with a selection of smart town flats and houses. *(Photograph 2011 L.R. Williams)*

THE SALTISFORD

THE GAS WORKS in the Saltisford started producing in 1822 and was one of the oldest surviving gas works in the country (possibly the world). To avoid recognition by raiding German bombers during the Second World War, the word 'Warwick' over the top had to be painted out. Production ceased in 1954 after new pipelines were laid to carry gas from Leamington Spa to Warwick. In

the early 1950s, when coal was rationed, local people were allowed to purchase the coke which formed the residue of coal for a small charge. It was not unusual to see people pushing old prams and trolleys in which to collect the coke. *(Photograph 1985) (PH449/569 Warwickshire County Council. Images held at Warwickshire County Record Office)*

THE GASOMETER, A distinctive part of Warwick's skyline, has long since been dismantled and replaced with a development of flats just off the Saltisford now called Ansells Way. The original office still survives, with its two octagonal buildings on either side of an imposing white structure. Paradoxically, while Warwick is now an affluent town, some fine old buildings like this one have long been empty and left to fall into disrepair. Described by a councillor as 'a blight on the town', the building has remained boarded up for several years, although during that time it did get a fresh coat of paint. The former gasworks, a listed building, was once occupied by Potterton's (boiler makers), George Waller (builders) and was bought by Laurence Gould (agricultural advisors) for £167,000 in January 1985. *(Photograph 2007 L.R. Williams)*

THE SALTISFORD

NOT ONLY HAS the former gasworks been allowed to deteriorate, but another historic building on this road has fallen into ruin. St Michael's Church and Leper Hospital was described by Leyland in 1538 as 'much in ruin and taken for a free chapel.' *The History of Warwickshire* records it was still in use in 1545 and provided hospitality with a weekly distribution of 8*d*, and the provision of four beds for poor men in the care of a poor woman who received 8*d* per week for attending them.

The remains of this redundant but historically significant building were incorporated into an eighteenth-century cottage next door and included parts of the stone walls, west gable end and an early fifteenth-century barrel roof in the cottage bedroom. The cottage has since been demolished.

Although some renovation work was carried out to restore the church, sadly it has again been allowed to fall to neglect, while the leper hospital has been wrapped in tarpaulin for decades. *(Photograph 1850s) (PH505/27 Warwickshire County Record Office)*

OLD COTTAGES HAVE been demolished and the site that was once occupied by Hutfield's Garage has been extensively redeveloped to provide a church and adjacent office complex. Behind the gable end of St Michael's Church is the new Church of Jesus Christ and Latter Day Saints. The first Mormon Chapel to be built in Warwick, it was completed in 2004. A member of the church, Gideon Wilkins, landed the role of John the Baptist in a 2011 film portraying the life of Jesus Christ, made by the Church of The Latter Day Saints, which was shot fifty miles from the Church's headquarters in Salt Lake City, Utah. Beyond the chapel are the new offices now housing the County Council Education Department, which relocated from premises in Northgate Street in 2007. *(Photograph 2011 by L.R. Williams)*

CAPE ROAD – PRISON

THE PRISON WAS built in 1860 at a cost of £75,000 and overlooked what was then open countryside. It was built to replace the existing Bridewell and gaol in Northgate Street. Built on a site of 10 acres and surrounded by a high wall, it held about 500 prisoners. Surrounding the outer wall was an open iron fence, between which were twenty-nine allotments. These were leased to cottagers in the surrounding area at an annual rent of £5.0s.4p. To the left of the prison was the Governor's House.

The prison comprised 309 cells, four day rooms, two yards for criminals, forty-three sleeping rooms, four yards and five day rooms for debtors. It included a treadmill which was used for pumping water for prison use. A grim reminder of past punishments was a stanchion with rings in the brickwork which was used to secure the hands and feet of prisoners who were the unfortunate recipients of the cat o' nine tails. It was demolished in 1934, although the Governor's House still remains. *(Photograph early twentieth century) (PH143/1021 Images held at Warwickshire County Record Office)*

HANWORTH ROAD AND Landor Road were built on the site of the prison. The striking blue-bricked Governor's House was converted into a public house in 1935, and closed in 1988. It was later converted into offices and apartments. On the opposite side of the road in Lower Cape Road is a more recent development of flats and houses. Building on the substantial site began in 2007. The land was previously occupied by Benford's, dumper-truck manufacturers who were established in Warwick for sixty years and employed about 250 people. After it was bought by the Terex Corporation in 1999, Benford's relocated to a site in Manchester in 2002. *(Photograph 2011 by N.P. Williams)*

GUY'S CLIFFE

THE CHAPEL AND ruins of Guy's Cliffe is situated on a steep knoll and overlooks the river Avon in a picturesque setting. Beneath the ruins is a cave where the legendary Guy, Earl of Warwick, retired to live a simple and monastic life after his return from the Crusades. Guy was a brave knight who slew the Dun Cow, a fearsome beast that killed many villagers, at Dunsmore Heath. After the dissolution of the chantry, the chapel was granted to Sir Andrew Flammock in 1547. It then descended with the rest of the estate to the Greatheeds, and eventually the Percy family who held it until 1946.

Opposite Guy's Cliffe, on a wooded knoll called Blacklow Hill, stands a monument which tells the story of dark deeds. It is here that the hapless Piers Gaveston, favourite of Edward II, was beheaded in June 1312. Captured at Scarborough and brought to Deddington and hence to Warwick Castle, he was tried by Guy de Beauchamp, Earl of Warwick, condemned, taken to Blacklow Hill and executed. Gaveston had dubbed the Earl the black dog of Arden because of his swarthy complexion and, as promised by the Earl, felt the black dog's bite. The monument erected by Bertie Greatheed records that he was killed by barons as lawless as himself. *(Photograph 1920s) (CR1125/94/10 images held at Warwickshire County Record Office, photograph by A.H. Gardner)*

THE CHAPEL AND sombre ruins of Guy's Cliffe House
has a romantic air when viewed across the river Avon.
Today, the ruins emerge from a sea of lush greenery,
in which they lay partially hidden. The Guy's Cliffe
estate was purchased by Mr Samuel Greatheed, MP for
Coventry in 1751. A famous visitor at Guy's Cliffe was the
well-known actress Sarah Siddons, who had previously
worked there as a maid in the name of Sarah Kemble. The
house was lent to the Red Cross as an auxiliary hospital
for sick and wounded servicemen from May 1915 to
December 1918. The house eventually passed into the
hands of the Heber-Percy family who left following the
death of Lord Algernon in 1933, but continued to have
an interest in it. It became a Boy's Home in about 1940,
and was purchased in 1946 by a syndicate of Warwick
businessmen who intended to convert it into a hotel,
however these plans came to nothing and the house
eventually subsided into ruins. An episode of Sherlock
Holmes, 'The Last Vampire', was filmed in the ruins in
1992, and during that time the house was even further
damaged by a fire that got out of control. *(Photograph
2011 by L.R. Williams)*

Other titles published by The History Press

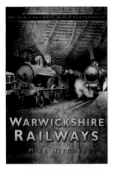

Warwickshire Railways

MIKE HITCHES

This is a fascinating account of the changes and developments which characterised this stretch of railway. The struggles and battles between the various railway companies – the L&B, TVR, LNWR, GWR and NWR – for supremacy over some of the Warwickshire branches are here evocatively depicted by detailed introductory texts to each section. This nostalgic collection will appeal to train enthusiasts, local historians and the general public alike and is an essential guide to an important part of our railway heritage.

978 0 7524 4933 3

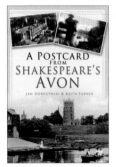

A Postcard from Shakespeare's Avon

JAN DOBRZYNSKI & KEITH TURNER

This book takes the reader on a journey in words and pictures through the five counties traversed by the Avon, using images from more than 250 postcards drawn from the authors' collections - many posted to friends and relatives by some of the innumerable visitors to the river and its world-famous associated attractions. It is a record of how the river and its surroundings once appeared, and how they were immortalised by earlier generations of photographers and artists, printers and publishers.

978 0 7509 4848 7

A Warwickshire Childhood: No Cakes for Tea

EVELINE A. HUGHES

This collection of memories follows a Warwickshire girl as she grows up during an era of huge transformation in Britain. Written to reflect her childhood impression of the world around her, this memoir reminds readers of the realities of everyday life in a bygone era. Illustrated with charming family photographs, this is a memoir which creates a vivid picture of day-to-day life in Nuneaton in the 1920s and '30s, including time spent in school, family holidays and the changes in the town itself.

978 0 7524 5162 6

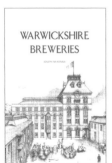

Warwickshire Breweries

JOE MCKENNA

This informative book provides an insight into the history of brewing in Warwickshire. It covers the story of brewing in the county, and charts the history of the county's licensed trade from humble beginnings – from the creation of a Common Brewery at Coventry in 1801, to the establishment of major forces such as Flowers of Stratford during the 1830s to the prominence of micro-breweries in the 1980s.

978 0 7524 3755 2

Visit our website and discover thousands of other History Press books.

www.thehistorypress.co.uk

The History Press